LIFE IN ANCIENT CIVILIZATIONS

The Babylonians

LIFE IN ANCIENT BABYLON

by **Martha E. H. Rustad**
illustrated by **Samuel Hiti**

Lerner Books
London · New York · Minneapolis

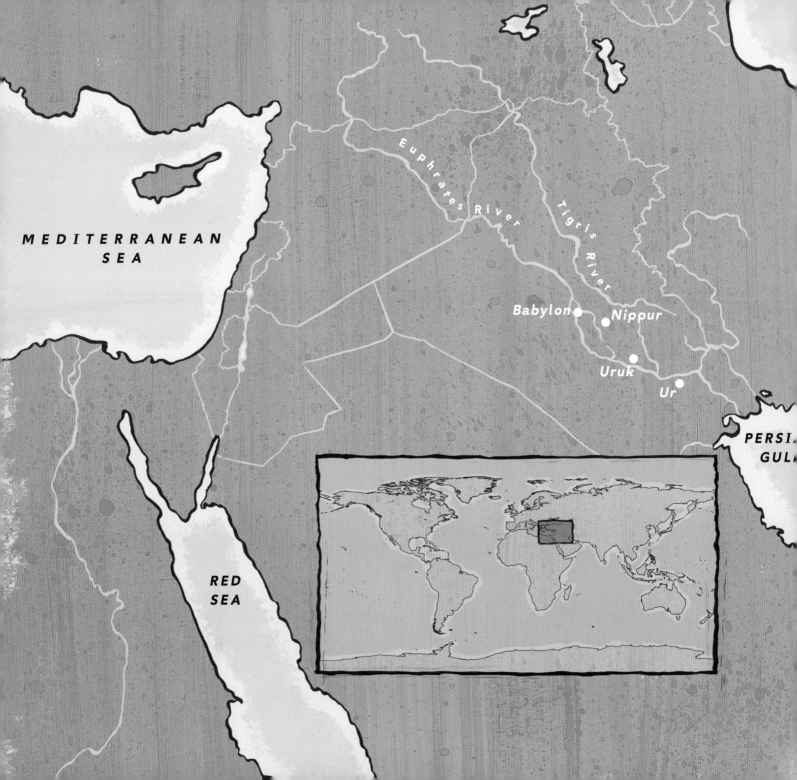

MEDITERRANEAN
SEA

Euphrates River

Tigris River

Babylon

Nippur

Uruk

Ur

PERSIA
GUL

RED
SEA

Introduction

Babylon is one of the world's oldest cities. People lived there as early as 3800 B.C. Babylon lies between the Tigris and Euphrates rivers in the Middle East. It is part of a region called Mesopotamia, which means "between rivers." Mesopotamia is known as the birthplace of civilization. It is also the land of the first cities. Some of the most important cities were Uruk, Ur, Nippur, and Babylon.

For a time, Babylon was the most powerful city in Mesopotamia. It was also the world's largest city. The Babylonians are known for their buildings, their writings, and their studies of the stars. The ruins of ancient Babylon are in modern-day Iraq.

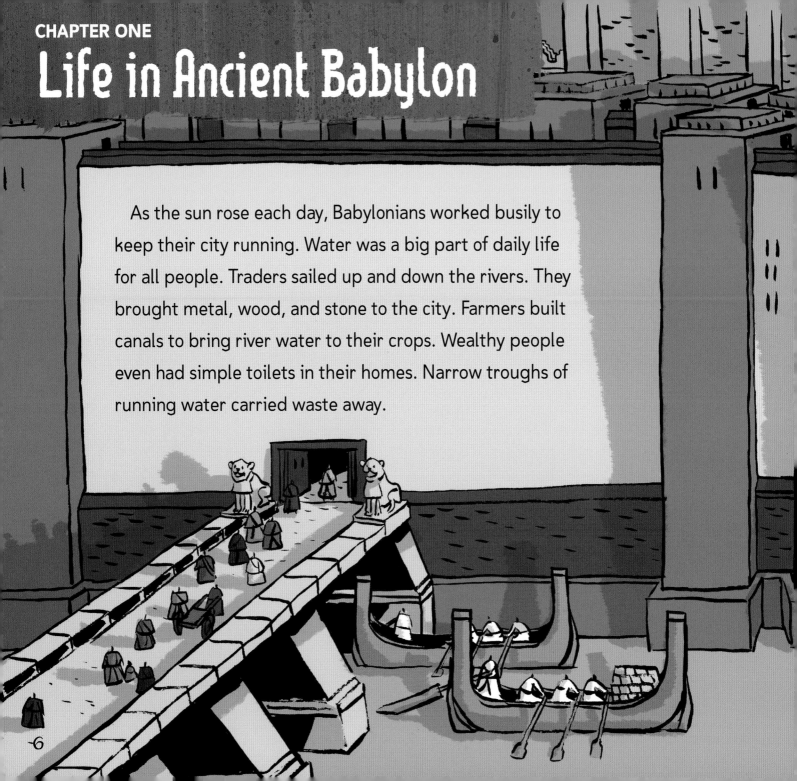

CHAPTER ONE

Life in Ancient Babylon

As the sun rose each day, Babylonians worked busily to keep their city running. Water was a big part of daily life for all people. Traders sailed up and down the rivers. They brought metal, wood, and stone to the city. Farmers built canals to bring river water to their crops. Wealthy people even had simple toilets in their homes. Narrow troughs of running water carried waste away.

River water mostly helped the Babylonians. But it could be harmful. The rivers sometimes flooded. Floods damaged homes and buildings.

Each Babylonian belonged to one of three classes. Free landowners were the highest class. This group included kings, priests, and soldiers. Landowners could practise trades, such as making pottery, working metal, or weaving cloth. Not all were rich, but all owned land.

Below this group were dependents. They were free, but they did not own land. These people often worked for rich landowners, temples, or the government. Some practised trades. Some even became powerful or rich.

Slaves were the lowest class. They were people who had lost their freedom. Babylonians captured some slaves in wars. Others owed money they could not repay. They were owned by temples, landowners, or dependents.

All classes of people passed through the Ishtar Gate (right). It was one of eight gates in the wall surrounding Babylon.

As many as 250,000 people lived in ancient Babylon. People often traded at markets near one of the city gates.

For much of Babylon's history, there were no schools. Parents or other relatives taught children a trade or craft. Children might have learned to make pottery or cloth. They might have worked on farms or helped out in shops.

When schools existed, only a few children went to them. In school, students learned to read and write. They studied religion, laws, and the stars. They trained to become scribes. Scribes copied texts by hand and kept track of them in libraries. No girls went to school. But some girls did learn to read and write.

Some tablets for writing were as small as 2.5 cm by 2.5 cm (1 inch by 1 inch).

Most Babylonians, rich or poor, wore similar clothing. They wove sheep's wool into large shawls. Babylonians also made linen fabric from the stems of flax plants. Colourful patterns sometimes covered the fabric. Both men and women wrapped this fabric around their waist and set one end over their left shoulder. They wore a short-sleeved tunic underneath. On their feet, Babylonians wore sandals or boots made of fabric or soft leather.

Women's hair was long and curled. Men grew long, curled beards. Both men and women wore jewellery such as earrings, necklaces, or brooches.

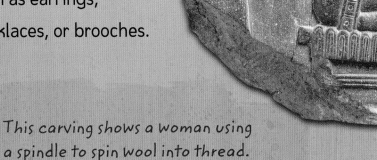

This carving shows a woman using a spindle to spin wool into thread.

Women spun wool from sheep into thread. Then they wove the thread to make cloth.

13

Babylonians ate two meals a day. One was in the morning and the other at night. They sometimes used reeds as straws.

Babylonians ate a variety of foods. They grew vegetables, fruit, and grain in fields. Women ground barley, a type of grain, into flour for breads and cakes. People ate cheese made from the milk of goats or cows. They also ate the meat of goats, sheep, pigs, and cows. Fishermen caught fish from the rivers.

This clay model of a house was found in modern-day Syria. An ordinary person in Babylon might have lived in a similar house. To stay cool, people often slept on the roof of their house.

CHAPTER TWO

Religion

Lama

Ellil

Scorpion person

Mushhushshu

Bull of Heaven

Lamassu

The word *Babylon* means "gate of the gods." Worshipping gods was important to all Babylonians. They believed their gods controlled everything, from the weather to harvests to health.

People across ancient Mesopotamia believed in many gods. They also told stories about imaginary animals.

People in different parts of Mesopotamia believed in different gods. The gods the Babylonians worshipped included Ellil, king of the gods, Ishtar, goddess of love and war, Nergal, god of death, and Nabu, god of writing.

Babylonians worshipped thousands of gods in all. They prayed to the gods of the sun, moon, and stars. They left gifts at temples for the gods of weather, rivers, and land. These gifts included food, money, and wine. People also burned incense and sometimes killed animals as gifts.

Marduk became the most important god in Babylon. He took Ellil's place as the leader of all the gods. Babylonians believed Marduk helped good people and punished bad people.

The dragon is one symbol of the god Marduk. The dragon's name is Mushhushshu, which means "furious snake."

The New Year was the most important religious holiday in Babylon. The New Year began in the month called Nisanu. This month fell during what is now March or April.

New Year's festivities honoured Marduk. Priests read a long poem about the life of Marduk. The king led a parade. It began at the temple of Marduk and went through the city.

Statues of gods were part of the New Year's parade. The statues were placed in boats so they could travel on the Euphrates River.

CHAPTER THREE

City of Mud and Clay

The Babylonians were skilled builders. But they had few trees, so they could not build with wood. They did have lots of mud, clay, and reeds from marshes. With these simple materials, they built homes, temples, and city walls.

This modern wall was built to look like the wall that surrounded ancient Babylon. An ancient historian wrote that the city walls were 26 m (85 feet) thick and 92 m (300 feet) high.

Outside Babylon, high, thick walls protected the city from enemies. Inside the city, another wall and a moat surrounded the main temples and some government buildings, homes, and businesses.

Babylonians often built buildings on top of the ruins of old buildings.

Babylonians used mud to make bricks for their walls and buildings. Some bricks were dried in the sun. The hardest bricks were baked in ovens.

Most people in Babylon built brick houses. But people who lived in marshes near the Euphrates River had simpler homes. These homes were made from dried reeds and mud. These materials are not long lasting. People often had to repair these homes.

This brick is from the ruins of Babylon. The writing on the brick includes the name of one of Babylon's kings, Nebuchadnezzar II.

Babylonians made many bricks in the summer. The hot sun helped to harden the new bricks.

A story from the
Bible says the
Babylonians wanted
to build a tower
tall enough to
reach heaven.
But God got angry.
To punish the people,
he made them
speak different
languages. They
couldn't understand
one another, so they
couldn't finish
the tower, called
the Tower of Babel.
A Babel means "a
confusing noise made
by many voices."

To enter the city, people passed though one of eight gates. The gates were decorated with lions, bulls, and dragons made of coloured brick. Babylonians built many temples from bricks too. The most famous was the Tower of Babel. It was a tall tower called a ziggurat. The base of the tower was 91 m (100 yards) on each side. That's the length of a football field. Stories about the tower have inspired many artists. Artists made pictures of towers that reached the clouds. But the real Tower of Babel had a square base. It did not reach the clouds.

CHAPTER FOUR
Babylonian Ideas

Many things we use every day were invented in Babylon. Babylonians divided the day into twenty-four hours and the hour into sixty minutes. The Babylonian calendar was also similar to ours. Twelve moon cycles of twenty-nine or thirty days made up their year. This lunar year was only 354 days long, so the Babylonians added an extra month every few years.

Babylonians did not invent numbers. But they were skilled at using numbers in addition, subtraction, multiplication, and more.

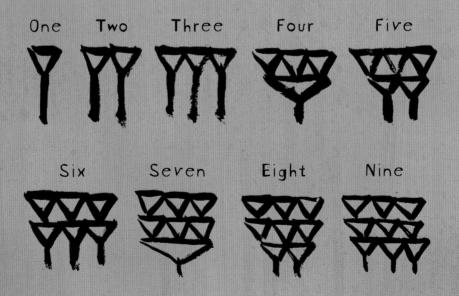

People in Mesopotamia invented numbers in about 3000 B.C.

Babylonians studied the skies day and night. They named constellations (arrangements of stars) they saw in the night sky. They predicted eclipses of the sun and the moon. Certain stars were linked to natural events. Babylonians believed they could predict the future by studying the stars and planets.

This clay tablet is a Babylonian map of the world. Babylon is at the centre. The triangles outside the circle stand for distant lands.

Theta Ophiuchi

Sagittarius
(teapot)

Corona Australis

Scorpius

Babylonians kept records of the
movements of the stars and planets.
They identified five planets: Mercury,
Venus, Mars, Jupiter, and Saturn.

In the Epic of Gilgamesh, Gilgamesh and Enkidu must fight the Bull of Heaven.

Cuneiform is the oldest kind of writing ever found. The Sumerians, who lived near Babylon, invented this style of writing. To write in cuneiform, people used a reed to make wedge-shaped symbols on wet clay tablets. The tablets then dried in the sun.

Babylonians used cuneiform to keep records. Some tablets have letters or legal contracts. Babylonians also wrote stories in cuneiform. They wrote poems, song lyrics, and prayers too.

The Epic of Gilgamesh is a famous Babylonian story. Gilgamesh, a king, was the main character. He and his friend, Enkidu, had many trips and adventures together.

This tablet tells part of the Epic of Gilgamesh. Clay tablets break easily and are often found broken in many pieces.

CHAPTER FIVE

Famous Rulers

The Babylonians left behind lists of their kings on clay tablets. The lists tell the great deeds of each king and other important events.

King Hammurabi ruled Babylon from 1792 to 1750 B.C. He put together a set of laws called the Code of Hammurabi. These laws are some of the oldest in the world.

Breaking each law had a punishment. If a farmer accidentally flooded his neighbour's field, he had to pay for the lost crop. If a son hit his father, the son's hand would be cut off.

The Code of Hammurabi has 282 laws. The laws are carved on this stone. The top shows Hammurabi with Shamash, the sun god.

Hammurabi is known for his laws and for taking over cities near Babylon. He also repaired the city's temples.

King Nebuchadnezzar II ruled Babylon from 605 to 562 B.C. He is famous for making Babylon a bigger and better city. He fixed canals that brought water to crops. He built another wall around the city. He also built the Hanging Gardens.

The Hanging Gardens of Babylon were one of the seven wonders of the ancient world. A Greek writer said that Nebuchadnezzar II built the gardens for his wife. They grew on the palace rooftop. Many plants, flowers, and even trees covered the gardens' many levels. Water was brought up from the Euphrates River for the plants.

The remains of the Hanging Gardens have never been found. Ancient writings talk about the site, but modern historians are not sure that it was real.

In 331 B.C., Alexander the Great took control of Babylon. Alexander ruled over a large area from Greece to Egypt to India. He planned to make Babylon the capital of his empire. But he died there in 323 B.C.

In 307 B.C., a new city named Seleucia was founded on the Tigris River. While Seleucia grew, Babylon's population went down. Eventually, Babylon fell to ruins.

Alexander (right) was born in 356 B.C. in modern-day Greece. He took over many lands. He travelled more than 20,000 miles (32,000 km) in eleven years.

CHAPTER SIX

Present-day Babylon

The ruins of Babylon are in modern Iraq. Some have been damaged by the Iraq War that began in 2003. But the ruins of the Ishtar Gate and the Tower of Babel still stand. A sculpture called the Lion of Babylon is also there.

Some things have been moved away from Babylon. Around 1100, people used old Babylonian bricks to build the city of al-Hillah, Iraq. In about 1900, scientists began to study Babylon. They found clay tablets, bricks, pots, and sculptures. They sent many objects to museums. The British Museum in London has a Babylonian brick. The Louvre in Paris, France, has the stone carved with the Code of Hammurabi.

This photo shows U.S. troops next to Babylon in 2003.

From 1899 to 1914, German archaeologist Robert Koldewey explored the ruins of ancient Babylon.

Babylonian ideas are part of the modern world. We divide years, months, days, and hours the same way the Babylonians did. We keep records by writing things down. We look at the night sky and see constellations that Babylonians named. Some of King Hammurabi's laws are used today. The ancient city of Babylon may be in ruins, but the ideas of its people help us still.

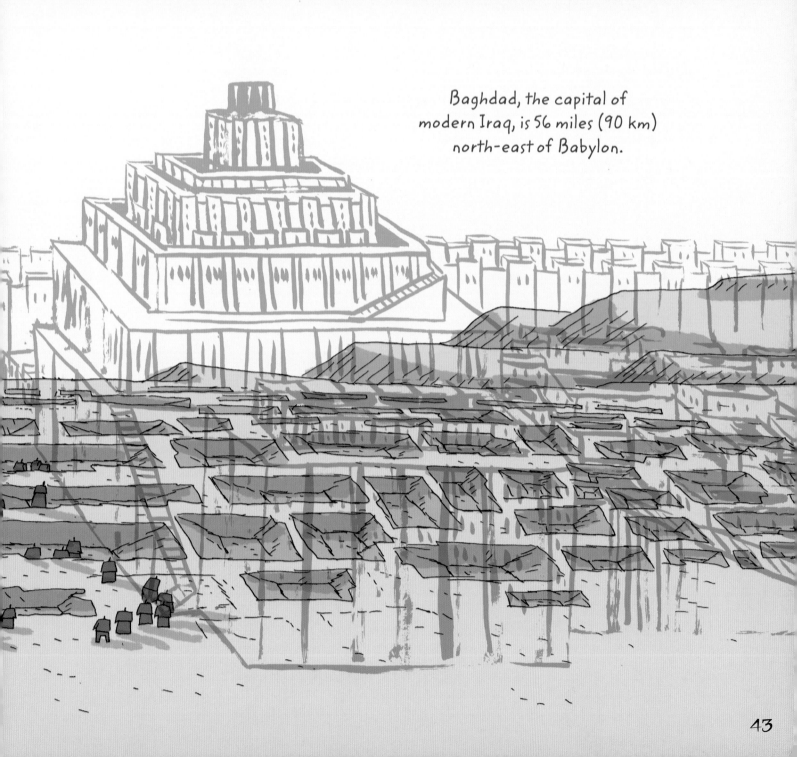

Baghdad, the capital of modern Iraq, is 56 miles (90 km) north-east of Babylon.

TIMELINE

1894 B.C. King Sumu-abum forms the first Babylonian dynasty.

1792–1750 B.C. King Hammurabi rules Babylon.

626–605 B.C. King Nabopolassar rules Babylon. His empire controls much of the present-day Middle East.

605–562 B.C. King Nebuchadnezzar II rules Babylon. He rebuilds the city.

597 B.C. King Nebuchadnezzar II conquers Jerusalem.

539 B.C. Babylon is overthrown by Persian ruler Cyrus the Great.

331 B.C. Alexander the Great takes control of the city. He plans to make it the capital of his empire.

323 B.C. Alexander the Great dies in Babylon.

307 B.C. The city of Seleucia is founded on the Tigris River. Babylon's population goes down at this time. Babylon is eventually abandoned.

ca. A.D. 1100 People use Babylonian bricks to build the city of al-Hillah, Iraq.

1899 Robert Koldewey begins to dig up the ruins of Babylon. He discovers the temple of Marduk and the Ishtar Gate.

2003 U.S. troops set up a military base on the ruins of Babylon.

GLOSSARY

A.D.: *Anno Domini.* This shows that a date comes after the birth of Jesus.

B.C.: before Christ. This shows that a date comes before the birth of Jesus.

constellation: a group of stars that forms a pattern

cuneiform: an ancient form of writing that was made by pressing wedge-shaped markings into wet clay

dependents: free people who do not own land

dynasty: a set of related rulers in a country

eclipse: the blocking out of the light from the sun or the moon

incense: a spice or other substance that is burned slowly and lets off a strong smell

landowners: free people who own land

linen: a cloth woven from the stems of flax, a plant with blue flowers

lunar: relating to the moon

moat: a deep ditch around a building or many buildings that is filled with water

scribe: a person who writes documents by hand

temple: a building where people worship gods

texts: writings. Babylonian texts were written on clay tablets.

tunic: a loose shirt that hangs past the waist

ziggurat: a stepped tower with a square base

FURTHER READING

Cowley, Marjorie. *The Golden Bull*. Watertown, MA: Charlesbridge, 2008. This fictional story tells about the lives of a brother and sister during a drought in Mesopotamia in 2600 B.C.

Samuels, Charles. *Iraq*. Washington, DC: National Geographic, 2007. Read about Iraq's history, geography, climate, and culture.

Steele, Philip. *Mesopotamia With Clip-Art CD*. London: DK (Eyewitness Books), 2007. Stunning clip art on the CD enables students to create their own illustrated projects and to understand the history of the period far better.

Wiltshire, Katherine. T*he British Museum Pocket Timeline of Ancient Mesopotamia*. London: British Museum Press, 2005. The timeline begins with the earliest inhabitants of the area between the rivers Tigris and Euphrates, who farmed, made pottery and invented a writing system before 3000 BC. It shows the rise and fall of the great empires of the Sumerians, Babylonians, Assyrians and others until the final conquest of the area by Muslim Arabs in AD 637.

Zeman, Ludmila. *Gilgamesh the King*. Plattsburgh, NY: Tundra Books, 1999. This is a retelling of the legend of Gilgamesh, a cruel king whose people asked for help from the gods. The gods created a friend for Gilgamesh to teach him about being human.

WEBSITES

BBC: Indus Valley
http://www.bbc.co.uk/schools/indusvalley/flash/ivtp_weblinks.shtml
A British Museum site, offering a moving timeline and the chance to compare the Indus civilisation with other ancient civilisations, such as Mesopotamia.

The British Museum: Mesopotamia
http://www.mesopotamia.co.uk/menu.html
This site features maps, stories, and games that let you explore life in Mesopotamia.

Gilgamesh (The First Superhero)
http://mesopotamia.mrdonn.org/gilgamesh.html
Here you can read part of the story of Gilgamesh, retold for young readers.

Gods, Goddesses, Demons and Monsters
http://www.mesopotamia.co.uk/gods/home_set.html
The people of Mesopotamia believed that their world was controlled by gods and goddesses.

Write like a Babylonian
http://www.upennmuseum.com/cuneiform.cgi
Type in your name and initials, and learn how to write your initials in cuneiform.

INDEX

PHOTO ACKNOWLEDGMENTS

The images in this book are used with the permission of: © Bill Hauser/Independent Picture Service, p. 4; © Bildarchiv Preussischer Kulturbesitz/Art Resource, NY, pp. 8, 12; © Erich Lessing/Art Resource, NY, p. 15; © Réunion des Musées Nationaux/Art Resource, NY, p. 18; © age fotostock/SuperStock, p. 22; © British Museum/Art Resource, NY, pp. 24, 30; © The Bridgeman Art Library/Getty Images, pp. 33, 34; LCPL Andrew Williams, USMC/United States Department of Defense, p. 40.

About the Illustrations

Samuel Hiti, who has a background in comic-book art, rendered the illustrations for the Life in Ancient Civilizations series using brush, ink, and computer. Hiti researched each civilization to develop distinct colour palettes for these books and create his interpretations of life in these cultures.

For JKR —MEHR

The publisher wishes to thank Eva von Dassow, professor of ancient Near Eastern history and languages, University of Minnesota, for serving as a consultant on this title.

Text and illustrations copyright © 2010 by Lerner Publishing Group, Inc.

First published in the United Kingdom in 2010 by
Lerner Books,
Dalton House,
60 Windsor Avenue,
London SW19 2RR

Website address: www.lernerbooks.co.uk

This edition updated for UK publication in 2010

British Library Cataloguing in Publication Data

The Babylonians : life in ancient Babylonia. -- (Life in ancient civilizations)
1. Civilization, Assyro-Babylonian--Juvenile literature.
2. Babylon (Extinct city)--Social life and customs--Juvenile literature.
I. Title II. Series
935-dc22

ISBN-13: 978 0 7613 5379 9

First published in the United States of America in 2010

Printed in China